SCIENCE SKILLS 1

1

MOVE YOUR BODY!

1 Match.

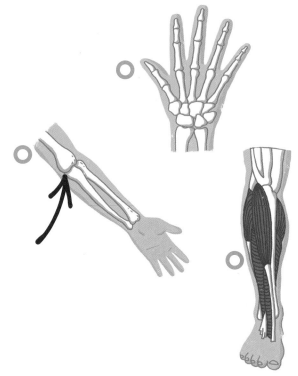

a joint O   O

b bones O   O

c muscles O   O

2 Find the words.

shoulder   elbow   ~~wrist~~   hip   knee   ankle

s	y	h	p	w	v	k	y	o
s	h	d	p	e	l	b	o	w
a	u	o	x	j	c	n	l	r
n	v	f	u	d	h	b	s	i
k	g	n	x	l	d	k	z	s
l	g	h	h	j	d	n	r	t
e	t	k	l	l	o	e	a	e
w	t	h	i	p	i	e	r	l
q	p	r	r	e	w	m	g	a

3 Colour the head, torso and limbs.

head

torso

limbs

4 Write *true* or *false*.

a My arms and legs are limbs.   true   false

b My ears are part of my limbs.   true   false

c My tummy is part of my torso.   true   false

d My eyes are in my head.   true   false

5 Complete the sentences with the correct number.

a I have got ___2___ eyes.

b I have got _____ nose.

c I have got _____ tongue.

d I have got _____ ears.

e I have got _____ mouth.

6 Look at the pictures. Look at the letters. Write the words.

a 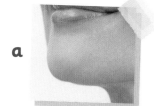   c h i n   h n i c

b    _ _ _ _   s y e e

c    _ _ _ _   e s n o

d 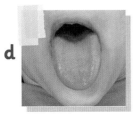   _ _ _ _ _ _   n t o g e u

e 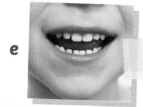   _ _ _ _ _   h u t m o

7 Read and draw the alien. Colour.

My alien has got three eyes and five ears.
My alien has got red cheeks and a purple nose.

**8 Trace the words. Colour
these parts of the body.**

hands

feet

tummy

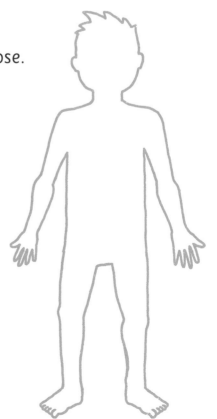

9 Look and read. Put a tick (✓) or a cross (✗) in the box.

a   This is a foot.   ☑

b   This is a finger.   ☐

c   This is a knee.   ☐

d   This is a toe.   ☐

e   This is a tongue.   ☐

10 Circle the correct option.

a *Joints / Bones* help you move.

b Your tummy is in your *head / torso*.

11 Match the photos to the correct sense.

see
smell
taste
touch
hear

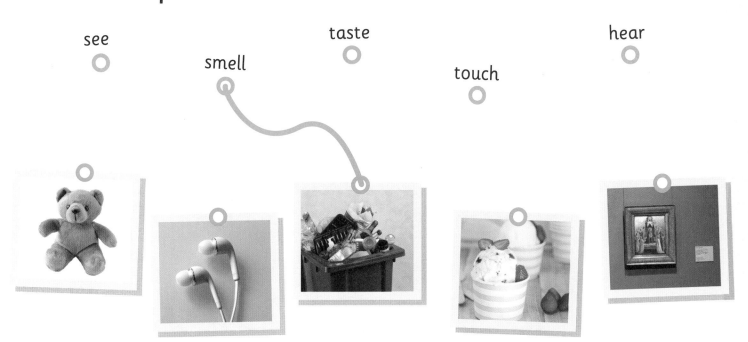

12 Trace.

a  touch

c  hear

b  smell

d  taste

13 Complete the sentences. Trace.

a I see with my eyes.

c I touch with my hands.

b I smell with my nose.

d I hear with my ears.

2 STAY STRONG, LIVE LONG!

1 Match.

carbohydrates

fats

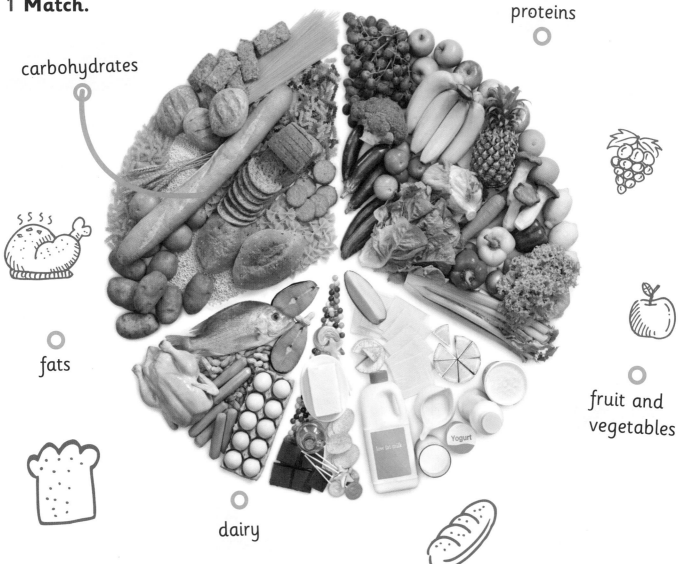

proteins

fruit and vegetables

dairy

2 Circle *fruit* or *vegetable*.

a — fruit / vegetable

b — fruit / vegetable

c — fruit / vegetable

d — fruit / vegetable

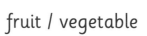

8

3 Circle the odd one out.

fruit and vegetables

carbohydrates

proteins

dairy

fats

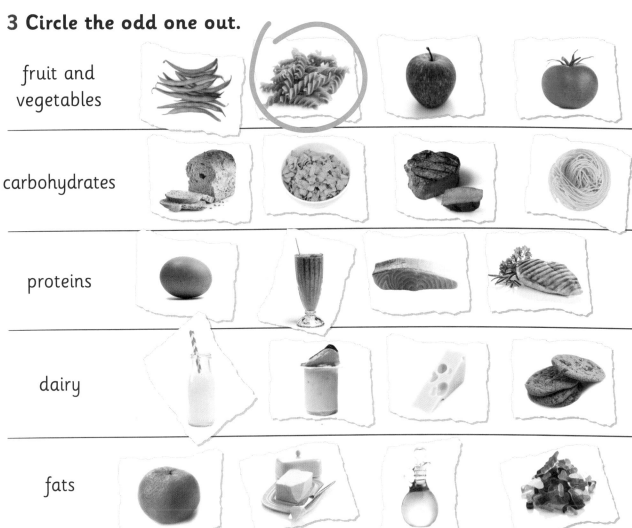

4 Trace and match.

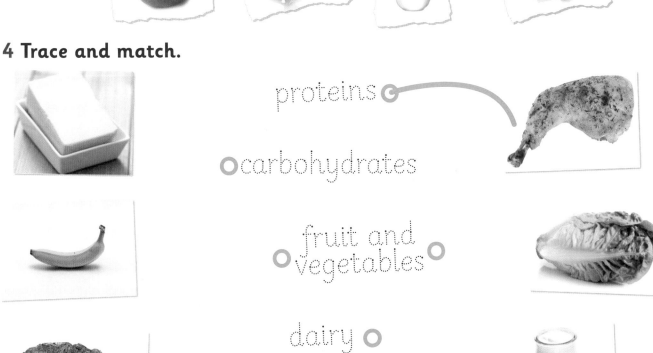

proteins

carbohydrates

fruit and vegetables

dairy

fats

9

5 Are these snacks healthy? Put a tick (✓) or a cross (✗) in the box.

a donut

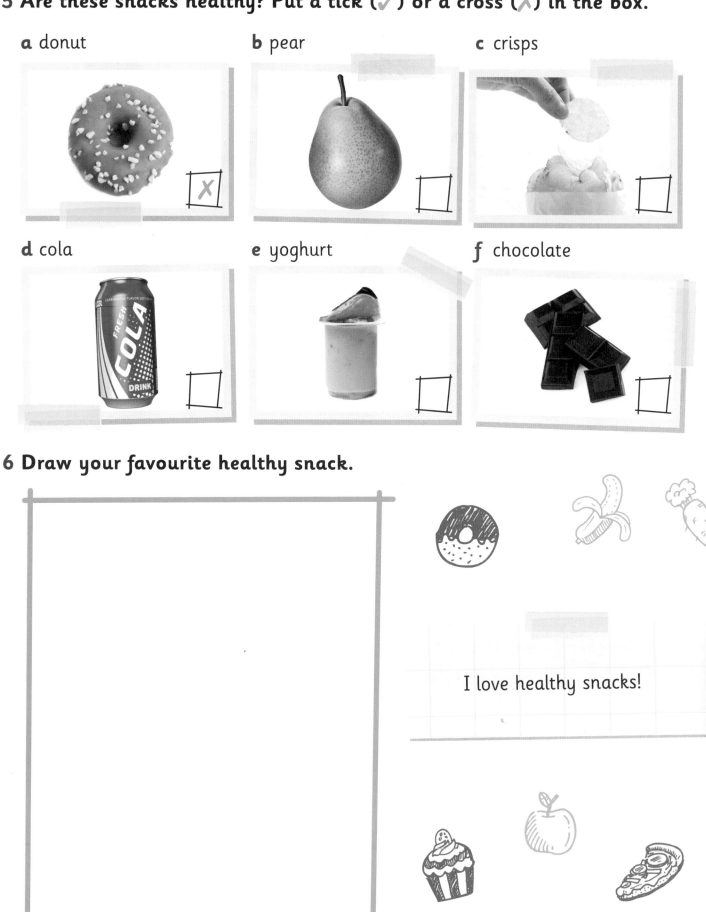

[✗]

b pear

c crisps

d cola

e yoghurt

f chocolate

6 Draw your favourite healthy snack.

I love healthy snacks!

7 Look at the pictures. Look at the letters. Write the words.

a  b r e a k f a s t   r e s b a f t a k

b  _ _ _ _ _   s n a k c

c  _ _ _ _ _   u n c h l

d  _ _ _ _ _ _   i d n n r e

8 Circle the correct option.

a Eat *three / four / five* times a day.

b Eat five portions of *fruit and vegetables / dairy / fats* a day.

9 Colour.

 healthy   unhealthy

10 Circle the correct spelling. Write the words under the pictures.

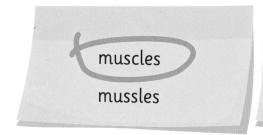

muscles
mussles

healty
healthy

heart
hart

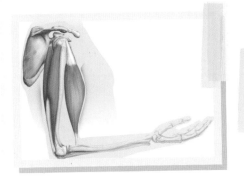  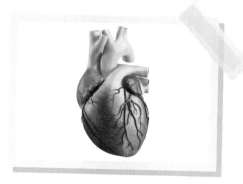

_____ _____ _____

11 Circle the correct word.

a I brush my *teeth* / *tongue* after meals.

b I have a shower every *week* / *day*.

c I wash my *hands* / *hair* before meals.

12 Match.

①

ⓐ

②

ⓑ

13 Read about Little Pasteur. Look at the pictures and trace the words in the text.

school

crisps

sandwiches

yoghurt

I don't like crisps. They are unhealthy.

I always bring healthy snacks to school.

I like fruit, carrots, cereal, yoghurt and sandwiches.

14 How do they feel? Trace.

a

angry

b

sad

c

happy

3 ANIMAL PLANET

1 Match.

a

b

c

d

farm   ocean   the Arctic   forest

2 Circle the odd one out.

invertebrates

vertebrates

14

3 Look and read. Put a tick (✓) or a cross (✗) in the box.

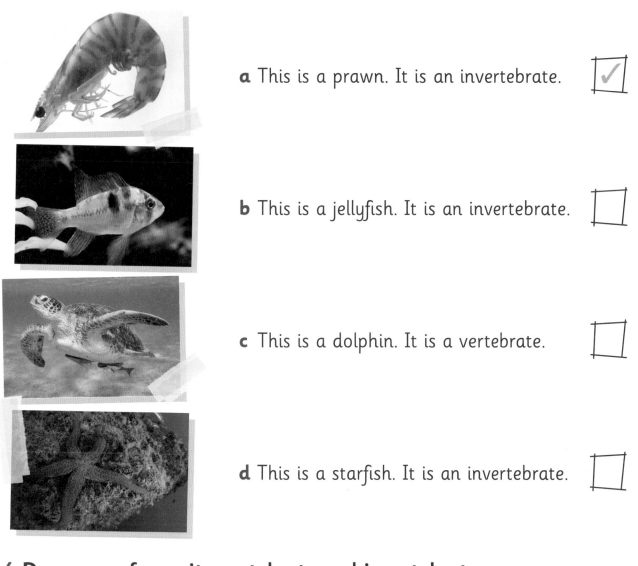

a This is a prawn. It is an invertebrate. ✓

b This is a jellyfish. It is an invertebrate. ☐

c This is a dolphin. It is a vertebrate. ☐

d This is a starfish. It is an invertebrate. ☐

4 Draw your favourite vertebrate and invertebrate.

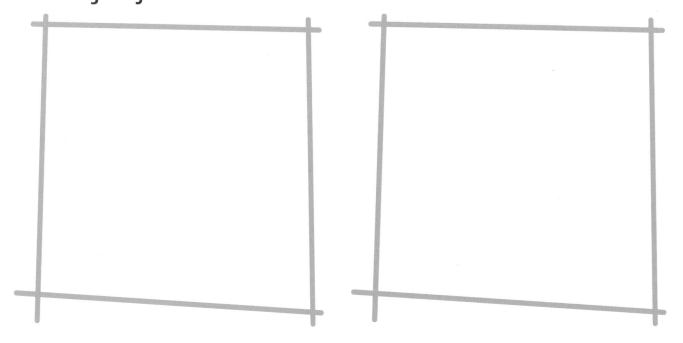

5 How do these animals move? Trace.

walk   fly   slither   swim

6 Draw the animals from Activity 5 in the correct place.

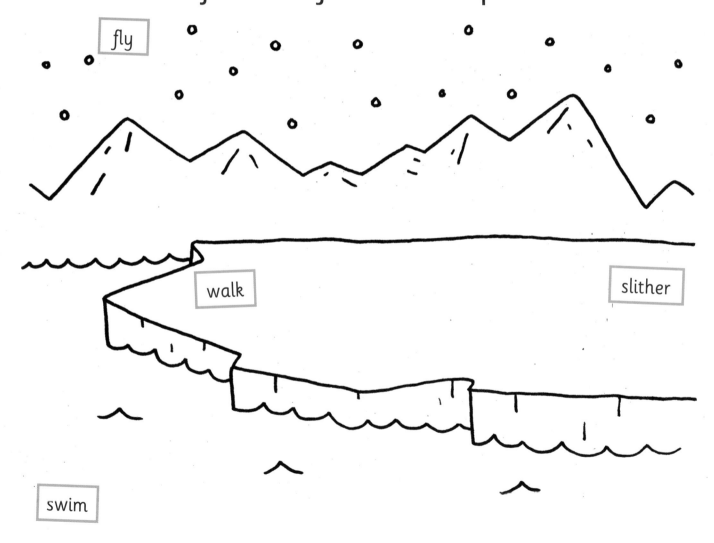

fly

walk   slither

swim

7 Look at the pictures. Look at the letters. Write the words.

a   f i s h   s i h f

b   _ _ _ _   d b i r

c   _ _ _ _ _ _ _ _   e l i r p t e

d   _ _ _ _ _ _   l m a m a m

e   _ _ _ _ _ _ _ _ _   h b i p a n a i m

8 Colour the mammals yellow **and the amphibians** blue.

9 Circle the odd one out.

mammal

reptile

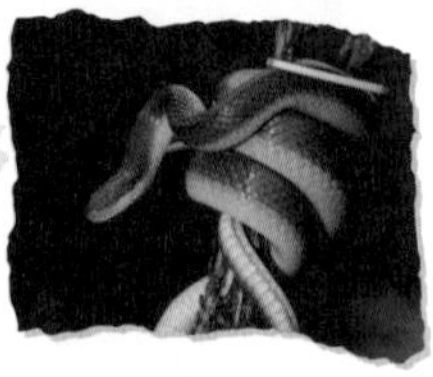

bird

amphibian

fish

10 Where do these animals live? Write.

~~badger~~ cow sheep hen owl fox

Wild

badger

Domestic

11 Choose a word from the box.
Write the correct word next to letters b–d.

Hello! I am a rainbow lorikeet and I am very

colourful. I am a (**a**) _____bird_____ and

I can fly.

I live in the (**b**) _____ and I can see

lots of (**c**) _____ .

(**d**) _____ , snakes and frogs are

my neighbours.

birds   rainforest   trees   koalas

12 Look at the photo. Circle the correct option.

a It is a *vertebrate / invertebrate.*

b It can *fly / swim / slither / walk.*

c It is a *mammal / reptile / fish /*
bird / amphibian.

d It *has got / has not got* any legs.

4 FLOWER POWER!

1 Look and write.

stem seeds flower leaves ~~roots~~

a _____roots_____

b _____

c _____

d _____

e _____

2 Label the daisy.

flower stem leaves roots

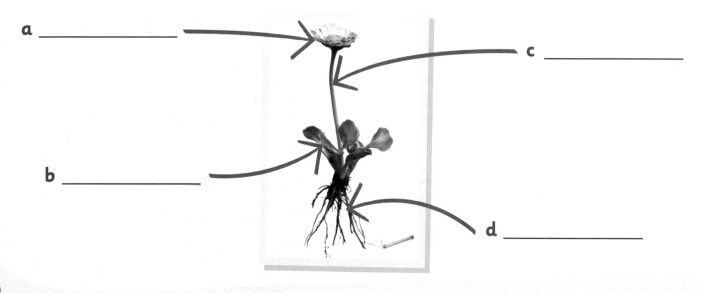

a _____

b _____

c _____

d _____

3 Look and read. Put a tick (✓) or a cross (✗) in the box.

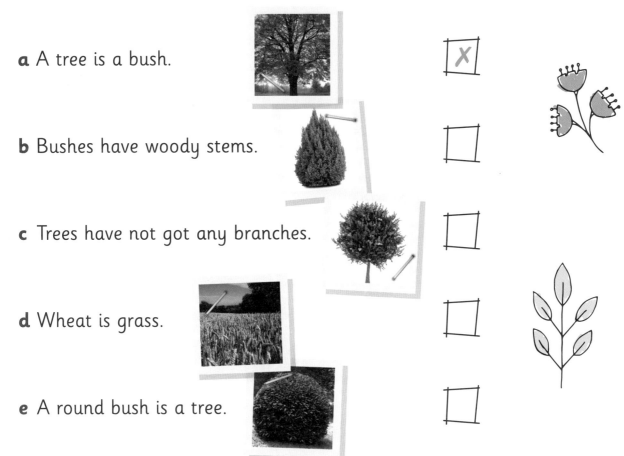

a A tree is a bush. ☒

b Bushes have woody stems. ☐

c Trees have not got any branches. ☐

d Wheat is grass. ☐

e A round bush is a tree. ☐

4 Complete the sentences.

bushes   grass   ~~trunk~~   branches

Trees are tall. They have a thick (**a**) ___trunk___ and (**b**) _____ .
(**c**) _____ have got a lot of woody stems.
(**d**) _____ is bendy.

5 Colour the cultivated plants green.

6 Look and read. Write yes or no.

a There is a farmer working on the farm. _____yes_____

b There are three hens. _____

c There are cultivated plants. _____

d The cultivated plants are lettuce, oranges and dandelions. _____

e There are some wild flowers. _____

7 What do we use these plants for? Label the pictures.

food   medicine   clothes   ~~furniture~~

furniture   _____   _____   _____

8 Match.

strawberry   cotton   pine tree   chamomile

9 What do plants need? Put a tick (✓) in the correct boxes.

a ✓   b ☐   c ☐   d ☐   e ☐

10 Write *true* or *false*.

a Plants need water to live.   true   false

b Plants need air to live.   true   false

c Plants can live in drawers.   true   false

d Plants need orange juice.   true   false

11 Which photos show children respecting plants?
Put a tick (✓) in the correct boxes.

12 Colour the bad behaviour red and the good behaviour green.

5 I'M ALIVE!

1 Look and write.

animal   people   plants

_____   _____   _____

2 Order the life cycle of a plant. Write numbers 1–4 in the boxes.

Plants grow.

Plants die.

Plants reproduce.

Plants are born.

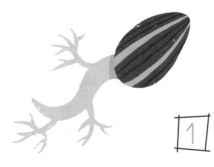   1

3 What do animals and people need to live? Draw.

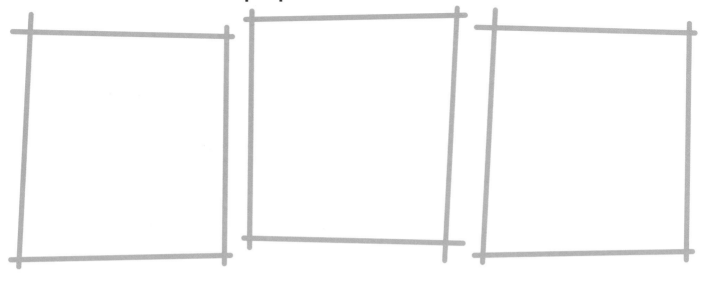

_____   _____   _____

4 Write yes or no.

a Plants need milk to live.   _____no_____

b People, animals and plants need food to live.   _____

c People, animals and plants need air to live.   _____

d Animals need clothes to live.   _____

5 Number the pictures and trace the words.

Animals …

reproduce.   are born.   grow.

6 Complete the sentences.

~~babies~~ girl boy born reproduce adults

First, people are born and they are
(**a**) __babies__ . Then, they grow into
a (**b**) _____ or a (**c**) _____ .
They continue growing and become
(**d**) _____ . They (**e**) _____
and have babies.

7 Circle the odd one out.

living things

non-living things

8 Circle the words.

reproducegrowbornairwaterfood

28

9 Look and read. Put a tick (✓) or a cross (✗) in the box.

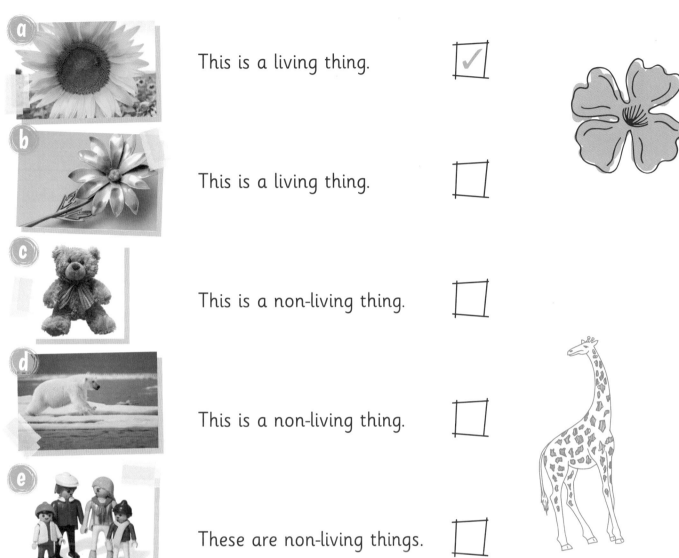

a This is a living thing. ✓

b This is a living thing. ☐

c This is a non-living thing. ☐

d This is a non-living thing. ☐

e These are non-living things. ☐

10 Complete the sentences.

living   air   water   non-living   ~~lion~~

A _____lion_____ is a _____
thing because it needs _____ ,
food and _____ to live.

11 What is it? Read and write the answer.

a chair

a gorilla

the sun

a sunflower

a

It is a non-living thing.
It gives you heat and light.
It is yellow.
You can see it in the sky.
What is it?
It is _____ .

b

It is a non-living thing.
It is made of wood.
It has got four legs.
You sit on it.
What is it?
It is _____ .

12 Find the words.

cloud ~~sun~~ rock water sand

s	a	n	d	q	a	w
c	o	y	b	w	r	a
b	l	t	e	x	o	t
j	m	o	s	f	c	e
r	u	s	u	n	k	r
a	q	p	c	d	y	o

13 Colour the living things green. Colour the non-living things red.

14 Look at the picture in Activity 13 again and read the questions. Write one-word answers.

   a How many people are in the canoe? _____

   b What is the man doing?   he is _____

   c How many tents are there?   _____

15 Draw a living thing.

6 FEELINGS LAB

1 Match.

a

b

c

○ I can help.

○ I am nice.

○ I am clever.

2 Circle the odd one out.

good choices at
school

good choices at
home

3 Look at the pictures and read the questions. Write one-word answers.

a Where are they?   in the ___kitchen___

b What is the mum putting in the fridge?   _____

c Is the girl helping?   _____

d Is the boy being kind to the girl?   _____

e Is the girl happy?   _____

4 Circle the super classmates.

a

b

c

d

5 Look at the pictures. Write the good choices in the table.

With friends	At school	At home
play fair		

play fair

get your
schoolbag ready

listen to others

be kind

6 Draw examples of good behaviour at school, at home and with your friends.

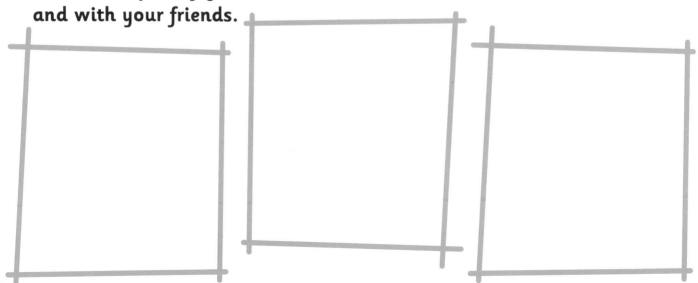

7 Choose a word from the box. Write the correct word next to letters b–e.

To be a good (**a**) ___friend___ you have to (**b**) _____ fair!

Always use kind (**c**) _____: *please* and *thank* you are the magic words.

Never be a (**d**) _____ and take care of (**e**) _____ _____ .

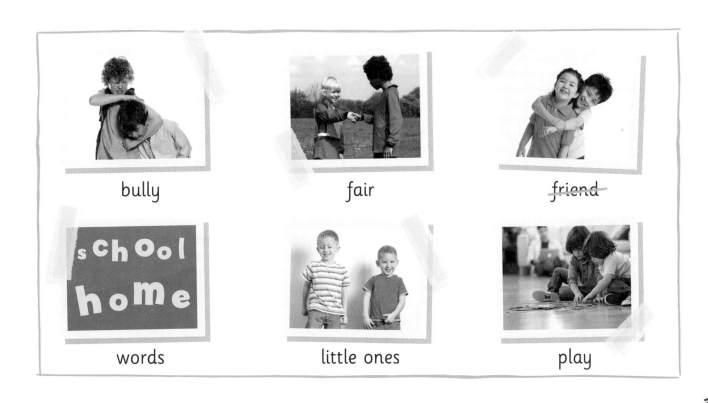

bully   fair   f̶r̶i̶e̶n̶d̶

words   little ones   play

8 Draw a friend. Complete the sentences.

kind   fair   thank you   helps

Name: _____

My friend is _____ and plays _____ .

My friend _____ me.

My friend always says _____ .

9 How do you help at home?
Tick (✓) or cross (✗).

a I make my bed   ✓

b I fight with my brothers or sisters.

c I get my schoolbag ready.

d I tidy my room.

e I keep calm.

10 Colour the good choices in the picture.

11 Find the words.

listen   help   share   respect

l	j	s	h	a	r	e
l	i	f	b	m	p	g
r	e	s	p	e	c	t
n	e	e	t	v	y	c
d	s	f	h	e	l	p
z	i	a	y	p	n	m

HOW DO YOU SAY ...?

Try writing these words in your own language!

Unit 1 – Move your body!

bones _____

joints _____

muscles _____

limbs _____

torso _____

hear _____

taste _____

touch _____

see _____

smell _____

Unit 2 – Stay strong, live long!

dairy _____

fats _____

fruit _____

vegetables _____

carbohydrates _____

proteins _____

breakfast _____

snack _____

lunch _____

dinner _____

healthy _____

unhealthy _____

Unit 3 – Animal planet

invertebrate _____

vertebrate _____

fly _____

slither _____

swim _____

walk _____

amphibian _____

bird _____

fish _____

mammal _____

reptile _____

Unit 4 – Flower power!

flower _____

leaves _____

roots _____

seeds _____

stem _____

bush _____

branch _____

grass _____

tree _____

trunk _____

cultivated _____

wild _____

Unit 5 – I'm alive!

be born _____

die _____

grow _____

reproduce _____

air _____

food _____

light _____

water _____

living _____

non-living _____

Unit 6 – Feelings lab

be kind _____

be nice _____

help _____

be honest _____

keep calm _____

listen _____

respect _____

tidy up _____

try your best _____

work hard _____